For many people, retirement is disorienting; they lose their sense of purpose and direction. Paul Damon's *Purpose-Filled Retirement* is full of clear and sage advice on how to find one's way in retirement. Damon avoids simplistic descriptions of retirement and simplistic advice. The picture of retirement that emerges is that of a rich and multi-dimensioned stage of life. It's easily the best thing on the topic that I have read. I strongly recommend it to all who are thinking about retirement, both those who are retired and those who are not—and to all those who *should* be thinking about retirement but are not.

Nicholas Wolterstorff
Noah Porter Professor Emeritus of Philosophical Theology,
Yale University
author of *Lament for a Son*

Paul Damon's picture of a biblical worldview of retirement is inspiring and refreshing. He encourages believers to think deeply and critically about this very important stage of life. Damon offers a powerful plan to align Christians with God's purpose for their lives. I have found this book to be an enlightening and engaging exposé on this very important subject.

H. B. London
Pastor to Pastors Emeritus, Focus on the Family
author of *Pause, Recharge, Refresh*

"You have plenty of grain laid up for many years. Take life easy; eat, drink and be merry." The world we live in calls this "retirement living." God calls it foolishness. If you're wondering when to retire, just ask

yourself what the expiration date is on your calling. I encourage you to read Paul Damon's book and rethink this passage in life that has become an assumed entitlement in our society.

Mitch Anthony
author of *The New Retirementality*

Purpose-Filled Retirement is a much-needed guide that gives the reader confidence and a clear sense of direction as he or she looks ahead to retirement. Paul Damon's book reflects the wisdom he has accumulated over the years counseling scores of people to carefully navigate their lives in such a way that Christ is honored.

Paul A. Kienel, Founder and President Emeritus
Association of Christian Schools International

Today we all need to be reminded of the fundamental call to seek first the kingdom of God and his righteousness. Here Paul Damon provides this reminder and shows us how we can master our own legacy in such a way that it can only be measured fully on the time-line of eternity.

Purpose-Filled Retirement represents not only a tender calling to turn our hearts to God, but also represents a fabulous prospectus concerning the assets God entrusts us with. It represents the finest life planning book I have ever read. It is a road map that will lead any believer to those precious words, "Well done, thou good and faithful servant."

Christian Thomas Lee
Concert Classical Guitarist
Collector of Fine Art

Purpose-
Filled
Retirement

Purpose-Filled Retirement

PAUL DAMON
CFP®, CLU, ChFC

credo
house publishers

Published in the United States by Credo House Publishers,
a division of Credo Communications, LLC, Grand Rapids,
Michigan. www.credohousepublishers.com

ISBN: 978-1-625860-13-2

Editing by Michael A. Vander Klipp
Cover design by LUCAS Art & Design
Interior design by Frank Gutbrod

Printed in the United States of America

First edition

Contents

Introduction

Retirement: Are You Ready?

Quick: What's your reaction to that question? One company has run a series of television ads that ask "people on the street" this question. Their answers vary, but most of these (polished hired actors) seem more than a little nervous about the notion. How does one plan so that the funds they have set aside will be enough for a retirement that could last as long as some careers?

Now, for certain personality types, this question's answer is as easy as if someone had asked them whether they wanted to accept a check for a million dollars. These people have an image of retirement that looks like paradise: long days of lazy recreation and enjoyment with no stress, no fear and no worries. These folks are not represented in the commercial spots. For other personality types, this question is fraught with concern: "That's a good question: Will I ever be able to retire? Am I doing enough? What will retirement hold for me?"

Retirement is typically perceived as the life stage that people attain as a reward for a lifetime of work: the pinnacle of one's experience as a productive adult. One's anticipation of retirement typically starts from the time one begins a career or learns a trade. How about you: Have you been looking forward to this event? How far away are you from it? Do you even want to retire? And when you do, what will you be retiring from? And what will you be retiring to? Or are you retired now and wondering if this is all there is?

This book is designed to do three things. First, to get readers to start thinking about some of the important questions that surround retirement. Second, to outline a biblical definition of what work and productivity look like, both for people directly involved in the workplace and for others who are retired. Third, to explain multiple options for individuals looking at retirement *and in retirement* and to point readers toward the option that best fits their situation. All of this is in the interest of encouraging individuals who are facing their retirement years to look at continuing their life of purpose in the face of changes in life circumstances.

My name is Paul Damon, and I'm the president of Family Capital Management in Grand Rapids, Michigan. The larger part of my career has involved helping people find their way toward responsible retirement from a financial perspective; however, over the years I have learned that retirement itself is so much more than building a nest egg to ensure that one can enjoy financial freedom over the long term. While that is certainly a critical aspect of consideration when building a career and planning a life at the end of that career, it is not the only aspect.

Many couples and individuals go into retirement thinking that generating enough money will assure them a peaceful and happy retirement. And for some that does happen. These are the individuals who have approached the end of their careers with anticipation of staying busy, of helping family and volunteering, of moving into the next phase of life with as much gusto as they had when they were at the height of their productivity.

Others, however, approach the next phase of life with very little planning. I've seen it happen many times; even those with significant wealth can struggle with the sometimes shocking difference in pace between their careers and their retired life. As a financial consultant, I make it my business to develop a personal relationship with each of my clients. I get to know them and their situations, and I hear this time and time again: "I guess I never put much thought into what my life would be like after I retired. I've done most of what I thought I would do during these years, and it seems like there must be something else to do, some greater purpose that I should be working toward. What do I do next?"

This book is designed to help you find your way toward a more purposeful retirement, a retirement that includes both times of leisure and times of busyness, times of relaxation (which is much needed and even therapeutic!) and times of pursuit. A baby boomer generation that has literally changed the face of politics, of medicine and of economics and has redefined what it means to age in the 20th and 21st centuries will settle for no less.

Thank you for taking the time to read this book. Thank you for considering what I have to say as valuable to your future. I hope this book encourages thought and personal reflection and perhaps provides direction as you consider what the next phase will bring.

I

Retirement:
A New Definition

Jim was a successful and energetic executive with a leading company in a demanding industry. He worked long hours and was fully engaged in his work as a leader in this dynamic, fast-paced industry. While he enjoyed his work, he very much looked forward to retirement, when he could relax, kick back, and do what he wanted to do, what he most enjoyed doing: playing golf.

While still engaged in his profession, Jim worked 60+ hours per week. Between that and trying to spend time with family and friends, there was little time left for golf. But when he could find time, he loved getting out on the links. Truly, it was his passion. Because of his success in business and careful investments he was able to retire early and begin his long-planned, well-deserved retirement. After his last day in the office, after all of the parties were over and all of the accolades proclaimed, Jim walked out of the building with a smile on his face and a spring in his step. He was ready to move into a new phase of life that involved fun and relaxation.

After Jim spent some time taking care of a few projects around the house, the weather was warming up and he was ready to pursue his passion. His retirement gift to himself had been a new set of clubs, and he was itching to get out on the links. He called his friends, set up tee times, spent time at the driving range and started what he had planned to do for years. His wife, knowing that for years he had passed on many friends' requests and sacrificed many beautiful golfing days to his career, sent him off with her blessing. This was it: Jim had arrived.

He spent as much time as he possibly could playing golf. He played with friends when they were available, joined many foursomes and made new friends at different courses and every now and again played alone. At first, the challenge of playing new courses and meeting friends was a rush. He was up before the sun and on the road. He was motivated, and he pursued his passion as many as six days a week. But as the season waned, he found himself playing alone more and more often. And as he played many of the local courses over multiple days, by the time he reached the back nine he sometimes found his mood starting to drag. After a few months, what had seemed to Jim like the ideal retirement plan became more and more an unfulfilling experience of emptiness and disappointment.

In Jim's own words, "When I was employed and working long hours under significant stress, golf became a respite from the stress. When it became all I did, it became boring and meaningless. I found myself wanting more from life, and wanting to give more." He started to volunteer more and play golf less, took several trips with his wife and became more and more involved in consulting with local businesses. While he still found himself on the links every now and again, this became more of a pastime that he pursued when his good friends were available.

Five years after he retired, Jim was in his sixties. Many of his peers were now considering retirement, but Jim wasn't content to sit on the sidelines anymore. He decided to swim upstream and start his own business. He used his experience and training to build a highly successful company. At this point he provides full-time employment for 60 people. And, more importantly, he is having the time of his life. Jim has found a new purpose; he is using his time, talents and treasure to make a positive difference in many other people's lives.

While 60+ hour work weeks are a thing of the past, he's enjoying being back in the saddle. And his golf game? Well, it's getting rusty, but he doesn't seem to mind. When asked when he will "retire" again, he smiles and says, "I don't know. I'm having too much fun!"

Retirement: A New Definition

In our day and age, how do we define retirement? Think for a few minutes about three different words you think of when you hear the word *retire* and write them down below.

To me, the word *retire* means:

1. _____

2. _____

3. _____

According to the *Merriam-Webster's Dictionary*, the actual definition of the word is this: "to stop a job or career because you have reached the age when you are not allowed to work anymore or do not need or want to work anymore." That definition carries with it the following ideas:

- To stop working or to withdraw from active participation in the working world
- To leave a place, position or way of life

To go to a place of less activity. Not exactly an exciting or encouraging description of the best life has to offer, is it?

What we see here is that the dictionary still buys in to the traditional definition of retirement. It speaks of one's moving from an active, productive lifestyle to a life of relatively less activity and little productivity. Is that similar to what you wrote in the blanks above?

The "traditional" model of retirement has been one of winding down, of ending, of withdrawing from life as we have known and lived it. The reward of the traditional retirement has been no more work, no more appointments or responsibilities, no more fighting morning traffic or sitting through rush hour after 5:00, and no more having to make so many vexing decisions or being under constant pressure to perform. And for many, such retirement is the goal of a working life—the reward for a lifetime of participating in "the grind."

While retirement certainly can mean a change of pace and a more relaxed weekly schedule, what has been added to the idea in recent years is a more secular worldview that focuses primarily on pleasure, relaxation and personal enjoyment. It conveys the idea of "I've earned the right to do whatever I want now that I have attained a certain age and saved a certain amount of money." In short, it includes a more self-centered focus than in past years. Jim's story is a good case study for what happens when one moves toward retirement with this kind of attitude.

When Retirement Doesn't Stick

We all know individuals like Jim. People for whom retirement just didn't seem to stick. Oh, it may have worked for a few months, possibly a year, but the days of leisure turned into days of boredom. Maybe the seeds for this kind of eventual discontent were evident at the very beginning, when the day of retirement came. When the much-anticipated day arrived, the person felt strange, as if they were needed one day and not the next—vital to the workings of a forward-moving organization up until 5:00 on a certain day, then obsolete at 5:01. It's for these people that we need a new definition of retirement.

Today's boomer generation needs more than what a life of leisure can provide, more than attempting to enjoy life while trying to manage a dwindling investment account, more than days of clicking the television remote or surfing the internet. For the generation that changed how people live and work in America, retirement needs to become a change of focus that allows one to follow one's new life purpose.

The reality is that a significant percentage of the population has adopted a secular worldview, and that carries into retirement. The secular worldview of life is characterized by four major themes: materialism, hedonism, individualism and collectivism. The two that most significantly impact this phase of life are materialism and hedonism. Let's look at each of these so we can understand how they contrast with the way Jesus told us to live.

Materialism is the love and pursuit of money and possessions. The primary purpose in life for the person with this focus is to accumulate as much wealth and as many possessions as possible. A bumper sticker you may have seen illustrates this well: "Whoever dies with the most toys wins!" The truth is, whoever dies with the most toys still leaves them all behind!

A materialistic approach to life is a shallow approach. We know from Scripture what Jesus taught us: "Do not store up for yourselves treasures on earth, where moths and vermin destroy, and where thieves break in and steal. But store up for yourselves treasures in heaven, where moths and vermin do not destroy, and where thieves do not break in and steal. For where your treasure is, there your heart will be also" (Matthew 6:19-21). Placing one's heart alongside possessions that can only break down and disappoint, or placing one's full trust in a financial portfolio that is subject to the ups and downs of the market is not only unwise but ultimately unfulfilling. Again along these lines Jesus asks, "What good is it for someone to gain the whole world, yet forfeit their soul?" (Mark 8:36). That's a trade-off that's simply not worth making—the temporary high of acquiring possessions against the eternal loss of one's soul, all because one's heart is ultimately in the wrong place.

Take a look at the sobering words of the Teacher of Ecclesiastes—likely Solomon, one of the richest kings in the history of the world—as he speaks about the accumulation of money and possessions:

> Whoever loves money never has enough; whoever loves wealth is never satisfied with their income. This too is meaningless. As goods increase, so do those who consume them. And what benefit are they to the owners except to feast their eyes on them? The sleep of a laborer is sweet, whether they eat little or much, but as for the rich, their abundance permits them no sleep. I have seen a grievous evil under the sun: wealth hoarded to the harm of its owners, or wealth lost through some misfortune, so that when they have children there is nothing left for them to inherit. Everyone comes naked from their mother's womb, and as everyone

comes, so they depart. They take nothing from their toil that they can carry in their hands. (Ecclesiastes 5:10–15)

Hedonism is the love and pursuit of pleasure and fun. This approach is typified by those whose goal it is to experience as much adventure as possible. They live for the opportunity to experience all the fun life has to offer. If they are still working, their time away from work is spent pursuing outside activities that make their life seem tolerable. If they are retired, they can now be fully engaged in all the entertainment and adventure they've been unable to pursue due to the time and energy constraints of work and family.

This approach, like materialism, starts out sounding exciting and fulfilling, yet ultimately even the most exciting experiences fall short. And, as age advances, the potential for checking off all of the experiences on one's so-called "bucket list" becomes less likely. For all of his wealth and influence, and for all the experiences he undertook to try to find meaning in life, again we look to the Teacher of Ecclesiastes, who clearly understood that experience is fleeting:

I denied myself nothing my eyes desired; I refused my heart no pleasure. My heart took delight in all my labor, and this was the reward for all my toil. Yet when I surveyed all that my hands had done and what I had toiled to achieve, everything was meaningless, a chasing after the wind; nothing was gained under the sun." (Ecclesiastes 2:10-11)

So materialism and hedonism are paths in retirement that may start out strong but ultimately fade away. The individual anticipating retirement needs to plan for other ways to find a new life direction.

Before we move into how one can determine a new life direction, find their purpose in life and comfortably and decisively move ahead in a new direction, let's take a look at what the Bible says about retirement.

2

A Biblical Perspective
on Retirement

For millions of people, the Bible is the source of life and light, a written gift from the God who created the world and everything in it, who sent his Son Jesus to save those who live in it and who, second by second, sustains the world to this very day. Millions of people look to the Bible in the morning as their source of inspiration and direction for a new day. Many of those same people turn to the Bible again at night to provide perspective and to bring peace to the end of their workday.

For those of us who follow Christ, God's very Word is there to direct our lives and bring understanding of what he would have us do in his world. We spend a good deal of our lives meditating on the stories and teachings contained within its pages. We attend church services where the Bible is explained and expounded upon. We join small groups and spend our Sunday or Wednesday evenings in the company of other people who are seeking to understand what God would have them do with their lives.

This is a word from God, passed down over thousands of years in the oral tradition until it was written down; this is a document that has been compiled and carefully curated and translated by people who have dedicated their lives to making it a book that everyone in the world can understand; this is a priceless treasure that people have given their lives to defend. What does it say to our current situation? What is God trying to communicate to us? What does the Bible say about retirement per se?

Nothing.

There is no reference to retirement in the Bible. Not one of the famous characters we know from Scripture came to a point in their still productive lives at which they decided to hang it up, get out of the rat race and take it easy. Adam. Eve. Abraham. Isaac. David. Solomon. The kings and the prophets. The judges and the shepherds. The apostles and the Jesus followers of the early church era. Did any one of them decide they had worked hard enough to earn a life of leisure? No.

Retirement is a new concept that came into its own only in the early 20th century, when the United States established its place on the world stage as an industrial power. Before this time, when the balance of families in the U.S. ran family farms, retirement was a notion that was difficult if not impossible to realize. Before the rise of investment counselors and wealth management professionals, people worked until they simply couldn't work anymore. Sounds rather like the individuals in the Bible we referenced above, right?

This discussion then begs the question: Is retirement a Godly concept?

The Life That Is Truly Life

Realistically, the Bible does address many retirement "factors" we need to consider as we move into the next phase of life. In other words, the Bible has a lot to say about how we use our time, talents and treasures, how we work, what we give and how we need to rest. A favorite passage in this regard reads as follows:

Command those who are rich in this present world not to be arrogant nor to put their hope in wealth, which is so uncertain, but to put their hope in God, who richly provides us with everything for our enjoyment. Command them to do good, to be rich in good deeds, and to be generous and willing to share. In this way they will lay up treasure for themselves as a firm foundation for the coming age, so that they may take hold of the life that is truly life. (1 Timothy 6:17–19)

Let's take a look at this passage and try to understand what the apostle Paul was saying to his young friend Timothy. To do that, we need only to start with the very first word in the passage: "Command."

What does the word *command* mean to you? Is it a suggestion? An idea? A thought? A "Do this if you feel like it" kind of word? No. I think we can all agree that this word is a strong imperative! In the original language of the New Testament the word Paul chose to use carries the sense of the word *charge*. Now, a good leader never asks those under his care to do anything he or she wouldn't do. So when Paul is talking here to Timothy, he is referring both to himself and the giving he has done as a regular practice and the giving Timothy is asking of his congregation. The meaning of "command" here seems to imply Paul's and Timothy's own willingness to come alongside congregations and deliver this message by their own example. The picture is of a pastor bringing a strong message of generosity and a spirit of giving and serving as he practices those principles himself.

Next, let's look at the cycle of movement in this passage. When Timothy leads by example and brings this message to his congregation, he points them toward the benefits of living in a generous way, a way that represents the generosity God has toward us. Those in this world who have more wealth than others are to use it in a way that will bless others. He points out the source of their wealth: "God, who richly provides us with everything for our enjoyment." That's a strong indication of the rationale for what Paul is asking of these people of means. God, who is the source of everything good, has given you everything you have. In return, your job as the recipient of these good things is to reflect the generosity God has shown in providing you with all these blessings.

Finally, let's look at the last part of the passage to gain a vision of the rationale for this command. What are the benefits of such action? Why would someone with wealth to spare want to have this kind of a generous heart?

We recall that Paul exhorts, "Command them to do good, to be rich in good deeds, and to be generous and willing to share. In this way they will lay up treasure for themselves as a firm foundation for the coming age, so that they may take hold of the life that is truly life." Paul is pointing his listeners toward a greater vision, reminding them that this present world and its material possessions are not worth their trust. He is giving them a greater vision, one that helps them understand that their possessions are given to them so they can make a difference in the lives of others around them who may be in need. And here the cycle repeats itself: God gives so that we may give to others. When God blesses us with what we need (Note: this is not always what we want or desire), our response is to be one of generosity toward others, whether we are a college student working part-time or the president of a multinational corporation. Net worth is immaterial in the face of this command to be generous toward others.

Paul then says something profound: "In this way they will lay up for themselves treasure as a firm foundation for the coming age" (v.19). What a wonderful, powerful truth. It is one found often in Scripture: that we can in fact "store up treasure in heaven." But the only way we can do that is to be generous here on earth.

Generosity on earth does not mean simple open-handedness with material possessions. It includes our wealth, but also our actions and our use of our time and talents. What a paradox: the only thing we can keep is what we give away. And everything we keep in this world will be gone in the end.

The implications are hard to understand. What will this look like? Will we have an actual "account" in paradise that is made up of everything we have generously given to others on this earth? No one knows, but Scripture is clear on this. There is a *direct* impact on our eternal experience based on how we live our lives here on earth. We are saved *by* grace *for* good works, which are a direct result of our attitude of thankfulness toward the God who extends his grace to us. Our good works (generosity) *will* have a significant effect on our eternal experience. Knowing this, wouldn't we want to direct as generous a portion of our resources as possible for the benefit of others so that we can reap the maximum eternal rewards?

The other benefit here, spoken positively for Paul's readers, is this: when you act in this way, you will begin to "take hold of the life that is truly life." It is once again Paul who states in Acts, "Remember the words of our Lord, 'It is more blessed to give than to receive'" (20:35), reminding us that Jesus had said this very thing while he was with the disciples. In following the advice found in Paul's letter to Timothy, we too will take hold of a life that is life indeed! In other words, we will get all the best of life if we use what God has given us in a way that reflects God's generosity toward us. What a powerful combination; we get the best of all this life has to offer, and we get maximum eternal rewards simply by being big-hearted and willing to give while here on earth.

How does this passage and its implications affect your attitude toward your retirement years? What are the implications of Paul's words for you today as you consider what you will do in the next phase of your life?

The Bible Still Speaks

Let's look at a few Scripture references to help us begin to understand what God is saying to his people about how they are to live their lives and conduct themselves as citizens of this world, whether as an active part of the workforce or some variation of that.

Attitude toward Money

"There will be terrible times in the last days. People will be lovers of themselves, lovers of money, lovers of pleasure rather than lovers of God." (2 Timothy 3:1–4)

"No servant can serve two masters. You cannot serve both God and money." (Luke 16:13)

Source of Talent

"But remember the LORD your God, for it is he who gives you the ability to produce wealth." (Deuteronomy 8:18)

"There are different kinds of gifts, but the same spirit. There are different kinds of service, but the same Lord." (1 Corinthians 12:4–5)

Use of Treasures

"For the love of money is the root of all kinds of evil. Some people eager for money have wandered from the faith and pierced themselves with many griefs." (1 Timothy 6:10)

"But store up for yourselves treasures in heaven, where thieves do not break in and steal, for where your treasure is, there your heart will be also." (Matthew 6:20–21)

Attitude toward Work

"There are different kinds of working, but the same God works all of them in men." (1 Corinthians 12:6)

"That everyone may eat and drink and find satisfaction in all his toil—this is the gift of God." (Ecclesiastes 3:13)

Attitude toward Giving

"He who gives to the poor will lack nothing." (Proverbs 28:27)

"The disciples, each according to his ability, decided to provide help for the brothers living in Judea." (Acts 11:29)

"But who am I, and who are my people, that we should be able to give as generously as this? Everything comes from you, and we have given you only what comes from your hand" (1 Chronicles 29:14).

God-Given Rest

"By the seventh day God had finished the work he had been doing; so on the seventh day he rested from all his work. Then God blessed the seventh day and made it holy, because on it he rested from all the work of creating that he had done." (Genesis 2:2-3)

"Come to me, all you who are weary and burdened, and I will give you rest." (Matthew 11:28)

"Blessed are the dead who die in the Lord. They will rest from their labor for their deeds will follow them." (Revelation 14:13)

Within these verses we begin to see patterns emerge. First of all, God is the one who is the source of work and everything good that comes from being a productive member of society. Second, as God is such a generous giver to all, we are to reflect God's character as liberal givers in the same way. The goal of the Christian, whether in the workforce or in retirement, is to reflect God's kindness onto others. The God who supplies all good things is the same God who delights in seeing the recipients of his goodness reflect that goodness to others. When those who have received so much move out of alignment with God's generous spirit and hoard his good gifts, their life steers into a different direction from the optimal life God desires for his people.

Whether actively working in a career or not, our attitudes should be the same. Our one goal in this life is to be more like Christ, to face every circumstance and situation in the same way Jesus himself would face it, and to react as he would. His kindness and generosity need to be our controlling aspect as we look at our money, our relationships and our abilities, and how those get used in the interest of expanding the kingdom of God.

Godly Retirement

Let's look at one more passage from the New Testament. This is actually a parable Jesus told that will help to illustrate the ideas we're looking at here. The story comes from the Gospel of Luke:

The Parable of the Rich Fool

Someone in the crowd said to him, "Teacher, tell my brother to divide the inheritance with me."

Jesus replied, "Man, who appointed me a judge or an arbiter between you?" Then he said to them, "Watch out! Be on your guard against all kinds of greed; life does not consist in an abundance of possessions."

And he told them this parable: "The ground of a certain rich man yielded an abundant harvest. He thought to himself, 'What shall I do? I have no place to store my crops.'

"Then he said, 'This is what I'll do. I will tear down my barns and build bigger ones, and there I will store my surplus grain. And I'll say to myself, "You have plenty of grain laid up for many years. Take life easy; eat, drink and be merry."'

"But God said to him, 'You fool! This very night your life will be demanded from you.

Then who will get what you have prepared for yourself?'

"This is how it will be with whoever stores up things for themselves but is not rich toward God." (Luke 12:13–21)

At first glance, the casual reader may be asking, "What's wrong with building bigger barns? If God has blessed this farmer with an enormous crop, why wouldn't the building of a larger facility be warranted?" On the face of it, the wrath of God against this prosperous farmer seems a bit of an overreaction, to say the least. Bringing this forward into today's context, it sounds a lot like what financial consultants encourage their clients to do on a daily basis. So is there some sort of a problem with planning ahead? Should we as Christians be more reliant on our belief in God's provision than on our savings accounts and 401K amounts?

All good questions. But the real question comes down to one of attitude rather than planning. While it's true that in multiple passages the Bible encourages total reliance on God and demonstrates his miraculous provision, we know that in our modern society, in order not to be a burden to our children or on society in general, it is wise for us to do some advanced planning and put away a portion of our income with an eye toward understanding that this is yet another way in which God is providing for our material and physical needs.

But let's look at the title of the story. The parable is about a "Rich Fool." Jesus used this story as an example of someone who has misplaced his priorities and is ready to keep all of God's good gifts for himself. This farmer is not unlike people who are encouraged to spend all their lives building a nest egg so they can spend their twilight years indulging themselves in whatever selfish pursuits they desire. The upshot of the whole story is that one never knows what's around the next bend. No one knows what circumstances a new day will bring. The exhortation in Jesus' parable directs us back to the passage that began this chapter for another look at Paul's instruction to Timothy: "Command them to do good, to be rich in good deeds, and to be generous and willing to share. In this way they will lay up treasure for themselves as a firm foundation for the coming age, so that they may take hold of the life that is truly life."

So, is retirement a godly concept? Yes, depending on how we utilize God's gifts in our retirement: our time, our talents, our treasures and our relationships. For one more exhortation to move us forward and to wrap up this discussion, let's look at Jesus' words in Mark 12:30–31:

The Greatest Commandment

One of the teachers of the law came and heard them debating. Noticing that Jesus had given them a good answer, he asked him, "Of all the commandments, which is the most important?"

"The most important one," answered Jesus, "is this: 'Hear, O Israel: The Lord our God, the Lord is one. Love the Lord your God with all your heart and with all your soul and with all your mind and with all your strength.' The second is this: 'Love your neighbor as yourself.' There is no commandment greater than these."

3

Retirement's Evolution

L et's look at the evolution of retirement over the last
100 plus years. The historical perspective on retirement was greatly influenced by the expected longevity of humans. Life expectancy from the early 19th into the early 20th century was much shorter than it is today. Thus, the concept of retirement didn't exist before the early or mid 20th century. Most people up to that point were self-employed (often farmers or crafts people) and could seldom afford to just quit working. Withdrawing from work was a gradual process that occurred with aging. With the industrial revolution, many people left the farms and went to work in factories, becoming part of a standardized system involving them and machines. Each was seen as having a finite productive life, and each was

retired from active factory duty at a predetermined time (for men, it was a specific age, regardless of one's health or desire to continue working). Thus, retirement was instituted as an event, a single point in time.

This concept of a mandatory retirement event was widely adopted in work settings, both in manufacturing and in non-manufacturing. As an example, airline pilots still today must retire at age 60, regardless of their years of experience or state of physical health. Thankfully, mandatory retirement ages are being eliminated in most industries, but the prevailing attitude about retirement is still that it is an event rather than a process.

Back in the early 1900s when most households relied on a single income, the male was the breadwinner and most jobs involved hard physical labor, people typically lived for less than two years after retiring from work. That statistic has changed dramatically as science, medicine and healthcare knowledge have progressed to the point that today retirees can look forward to spending 25, 30 or even 40 years in their retirement life stage. In fact, of all the adult life stages, retirement is now often the longest. And the majority of people who choose to leave the workforce tend to start relatively early; today, the average age of first retirement (defined as a separation from one's primary work or career) is between 57 and 58 years old.

Why do we use the phrase "first retirement"? The reason is that although many people leave their primary career at an earlier age, more are tending to continue their work life, either in a similar career with a new employer or in an entirely new career. Also, involuntary downsizing is having a major effect on retirement statistics. Many people are being separated from their service or employment because companies and government agencies are downsizing. These people are then responsible for re-establishing their career track, or in some cases starting a new one.

According to a 2007 Gallop poll on personal finance, over two thirds of non-retired Americans plan to rely on income from full- or part-time work after they retire. Why? Primarily for financial reasons, such as insufficient savings, fears about rising healthcare costs, doubts about the viability of Social Security, and the like. However, need is not always the determining factor. In some cases retirees continue working for reasons of personal self-worth (for identity, life meaning and finding purpose). Both of these factors result in many people now retiring two, three or more times before ceasing to work completely.

The Baby Boomer Factor

One major factor in the redefinition of today's retirement is the baby boomer generation: the roughly 78,000,000 Americans who were born between 1946 and 1964. The last of these individuals turn 50 in the year 2014. And if the statistic cited above bears out, a significant number of even these last boomers will enter first retirement within the next 10 years. Obviously, the vast majority of this group is already in some form of semiretirement or full retirement. What effect will this massive number of individuals have on the definition of retirement? What effect has it had already? We know that there has been and will continue to be a significant cultural and financial impact from this sizeable number of people moving through various life stages toward retirement.

Without question, the influence of the boomer generation has already dramatically changed the face of society in North America. The effect of this generation on the economic, social, financial and political arenas has been revolutionary as we have made the move from an industrial to a digital age within their lifetimes. The boomer generation has contributed in every way to the modernization and digitization of the world we know today. This generation has also been working to significantly influence the what retirement looks like.

Baby boomers have changed the rules of every adult life stage. The pre-1946 model was linear; first was the education stage, which began in early childhood and continued through high school and possibly through college. Next was the work stage, which began as soon as the education stage ended and ran continuously until retirement. Finally came the last phase, the leisure phase. This stage was the time of life when one was allowed to relax, enjoy their leisure time with family and friends and wait for their eternal relocation.

Today our lives are much more cyclical than linear. The boomers' life stages for both men and women often include education, career, marriage, parenting, empty nesting, grandparenting and retirement—and not necessarily in that order. Today, the adult lifestyle includes recurring and often overlapping periods of education, work, leisure, reeducation, career change and multiple retirements. Because of the complexity of this connected age, life today is much more circular than it is linear. Today the pattern of our adult lives is far less predictable and often much more interesting and challenging than those of our parents and grandparents. What's more, our children's and grandchildren's life patterns are likely to be even more varied and adventurous than our own.

Not Your Father's Retirement Plan

So what is the accurate definition of retirement today? A good friend of mine provided this definition: "Retirement is the time in life where you take off the old tires, put on new ones, and just keep right on rolling."

I submit that today's retirement can be defined in an infinite number of ways, that our options in retirement are limited only by our imagination, our health and our resources. Today's retirees tend to use terms like "discovery," "opportunity," "age of richness," and many other descriptors of a new life stage characterized by the themes of

1. Personal exploration and growth

2. The need to stay physically active and mentally stimulated

3. The idea that "work" will continue to be important, both for financial reasons and as a way to provide life with meaning and structure.

In fact, the word *retirement* is no longer an accurate descriptor for this life stage. Terms being used today include "rewirement," "refirement," "protirement," "third age," "third quarter," and "second half." The purpose of our retirement is to continue (or maybe to begin) to live life to the fullest, not to retreat from a life of productivity and usefulness.

To take yet another example from the pages of Scripture, let's look at the life of Moses. Saved from the evil of the Egyptian purge of male Hebrew babies by the grace of God and a devout mother, he was rescued by an Egyptian princess and adopted into her court (Exodus 2:10). Here's the story from Exodus 2:

> Now a man of the tribe of Levi married a Levite woman, and she became pregnant and gave birth to a son. When she saw that he was a fine child,

she hid him for three months. But when she could hide him no longer, she got a papyrus basket for him and coated it with tar and pitch. Then she placed the child in it and put it among the reeds along the bank of the Nile. His sister stood at a distance to see what would happen to him.

Then Pharaoh's daughter went down to the Nile to bathe, and her attendants were walking along the riverbank. She saw the basket among the reeds and sent her female slave to get it. She opened it and saw the baby. He was crying, and she felt sorry for him. "This is one of the Hebrew babies," she said.

Then his sister asked Pharaoh's daughter, "Shall I go and get one of the Hebrew women to nurse the baby for you?"

"Yes, go," she answered. So the girl went and got the baby's mother. Pharaoh's daughter said to her, "Take this baby and nurse him for me, and I will pay you." So the woman took the baby and nursed him. When the child grew older, she took him to Pharaoh's daughter and he became her son. She named him Moses, saying, "I drew him out of the water."

For the first 40 years of his life, Moses was educated in the finest Egyptian courts. He lived among the very people who had imprisoned and oppressed his ethnic— and his actual—family. He lived as a member of the Egyptian royal family and was given every opportunity and advantage of a young man in that position.

But evidently he had been apprised of his humble roots, because in the next few verses look what happens to move Moses into Phase 2 of his life, beginning at age 40:

> One day, after Moses had grown up, he went out to where his own people were and watched them at their hard labor. He saw an Egyptian beating a Hebrew, one of his own people. Looking this way and that and seeing no one, he killed the Egyptian and hid him in the sand. The next day he went out and saw two Hebrews fighting. He asked the one in the wrong, "Why are you hitting your fellow Hebrew?"

The man said, "Who made you ruler and judge over us? Are you thinking of killing me as you killed the Egyptian?" Then Moses was afraid and thought, "What I did must have become known."

When Pharaoh heard of this, he tried to kill Moses, but Moses fled from Pharaoh and went to live in Midian, where he sat down by a well. Now a priest of Midian had seven daughters, and they came to draw water and fill the troughs to water their father's flock. Some shepherds came along and drove them away, but Moses got up and came to their rescue and watered their flock.

When the girls returned to Reuel their father, he asked them, "Why have you returned so early today?"

They answered, "An Egyptian rescued us from the shepherds. He even drew water for us and watered the flock."

"And where is he?" Reuel asked his daughters. "Why did you leave him? Invite him to have something to eat."

Moses agreed to stay with the man, who gave his daughter Zipporah to Moses in marriage. Zipporah gave birth to a son, and Moses named him Gershom, saying, "I have become a foreigner in a foreign land."

Fear of Pharaoh drove Moses to the next phase of his life: that of being a shepherd and a family man in a faraway land. After spending the first 40 years of his life in an intensively privileged situation, he now finds himself watching sheep and wandering the countryside in virtual obscurity. There must have been times, sleeping among the sheep, when images of his previous life flashed before his mind. "How did I get here?" he must have asked himself. "With all the education I have, how is it I am here among the sheep with my family so far away?" But all the while God was preparing Moses for the third phase of his life, which wouldn't start until the age of 80. We continue in Exodus 2 and 3:

During that long period, the king of Egypt died. The Israelites groaned in their slavery and cried out, and their cry for help because of their slavery went up to God. God heard their groaning and he remembered his covenant with Abraham, with Isaac and with Jacob. So God looked on the Israelites and was concerned about them.

Now Moses was tending the flock of Jethro his father-in-law, the priest of Midian, and he led the flock to the far side of the wilderness and came to Horeb, the mountain of God. There the angel of the LORD appeared to him in flames of fire from within a bush. Moses saw that though the bush was on fire it did not burn up. So Moses thought, "I will go over and see this strange sight—why the bush does not burn up."

When the LORD saw that he had gone over to look, God called to him from within the bush, "Moses! Moses!"

And Moses said, "Here I am."

"Do not come any closer," God said. "Take off your sandals, for the place where you are standing is holy ground." Then he said, "I am the God of your father, the God of Abraham, the God of Isaac and the God of Jacob." At this, Moses hid his face, because he was afraid to look at God.

The LORD said, "I have indeed seen the misery of my people in Egypt. I have heard them crying out because of their slave drivers, and I am concerned about their suffering. So I have come down to rescue them from the hand of the Egyptians and to bring them up out of that land into a good and spacious land, a land flowing with milk and honey—the home of the Canaanites, Hittites, Amorites, Perizzites, Hivites and Jebusites. And now the cry of the Israelites has reached me, and I have seen the way the Egyptians are oppressing them. So now, go. I am sending you to Pharaoh to bring my people the Israelites out of Egypt."

But Moses said to God, "Who am I that I should go to Pharaoh and bring the Israelites out of Egypt?"

And God said, "I will be with you. And this will be the sign to you that it is I who have sent you: When you have brought the people out of Egypt, you will worship God on this mountain."

Remember, this is Moses at the age of 80. With the burning bush and God's call on his life to go back to

Pharaoh, he was able to perceive the path on which God had been leading him all his life. Despite his protests that he was not God's man for the job, Moses moved ahead and found his life's true purpose when most of his peers were relegating themselves to the proverbial rocking chair. His fame in the annals of history, and the way he served as the conduit of God's message to the people of Israel and Egypt may be attributed to his movement toward God's purpose much later in life, as a relatively old man.

As you approach your own retirement, do you feel a similar call on your life? A call to a new direction, a new sense of purpose? What is the burning bush in your experience: the birth of a grandchild or grandchildren and the opportunity to influence their lives? An opportunity to minister to others in a church setting or in some other volunteer operation? The chance to pursue a long-neglected passion that will bring order or beauty or music or art or some other contribution to the world? What gifts and abilities and educational opportunities has God given you that have prepared you for this next phase of life? How are you, like Moses, uniquely gifted to make a difference in the lives of others?

Moses' most remarkable contributions to history happened in the last third of his life. He spent his last 40 years in the passionate pursuit of what God had planned for him long before the time of his adoption by an Egyptian princess a full 80 years earlier. None of us can likely look forward to a life of action until we turn 120 (nor would most of us want to live that long!), but think about it: How can Moses' story inspire you to pursue a life of purpose after you leave behind your first career?

If you'd like to do some further study on this idea, consider the life of Joshua, who at 85 years old was still vigorous and ready to fight for his God:

> "Now then, just as the LORD promised, he has kept me alive for forty-five years since the time he said this to Moses, while Israel moved about in the wilderness. So here I am today, eighty-five years old! I am still as strong today as the day Moses sent me out; I'm just as vigorous to go out to battle now as I was then. Now give me this hill country that the LORD promised me that day. You yourself heard then that the Anakites were there and their cities were large and fortified, but, the

LORD helping me, I will drive them out just as he said." (Joshua 14:10–12)

See Joshua chapters 1–14 for the whole fascinating study.

Again, how can the lives of these men, who were so inspired by God, also inspire you to a new chapter of acting purposely for God as you approach your retirement years?

4

Living Life to the Fullest and Myths of Retirement

How then, do we live life to the fullest in retirement? The short answer is this: by pursuing God's dreams for our life.

But how does one go about approaching this pursuit? How can a person whose entire life has been taken up by the busyness of a career, perhaps raising a family and the incredible time and expense that entails, paying a mortgage and utilities and being an active and engaged member of today's society figure out what God has put in his or her heart to do in retirement? Many in this situation have never had the time to slow down long enough to consider this.

Consider the story of Jim in the first chapter. He was convinced, for however short a time, that golf was his calling. He pursued it with a passion until it began to lose its luster. That's when he found his true calling—to improve the lives of others by using his God-given talents and skills in the creation of a new business. Through finding that passion he was able to live a life that suited his talents and interests, while also helping 60 people find meaningful full-time work. Consider also the story of Moses in the last chapter. He found his life's calling when God pointed out to him that he had been preparing him for this role for 80 years. There was no other Hebrew in all the world who was better equipped to face the pharaoh than was Moses. And once God was able to convince Moses of that fact, he found his true life's purpose and, empowered by the God who had equipped him for the task, changed the course of history.

What has God placed on your heart? How do we know what God has *made* us to do, not just what we are being *paid* to do? Pursuing our dreams, our goals and our life purpose provides our focus for retirement. But first we must discover our dreams.

In some cases we have suppressed our dreams for so long that we aren't even aware of them. Sometimes these dreams are long-held desires or life goals that have always been with us—a "bucket list" of sorts. Maybe it's a matter of developing dreams or goals aimed in the direction of getting to know ourselves better—our strengths, our motivators, our joys, our passions. Once the dreams are identified, our challenge is to translate them into a retirement life-plan that will bring meaning to our lives and result in satisfaction and fulfillment.

To begin to tackle this idea of following our life dreams, let's first look at the various practical phases of today's retirement planning. The busyness of career will simply be replaced by the busyness of trying to manage money if there is not enough to live on comfortably after one's initial retirement.

Why is retirement planning so important? Some people, particularly the boomers we've been talking about, will be living in their retirement life stage for as long as they were in the workplace. For many, that's 20 to 30 years or more. So when is the right time to plan for retirement? No schedule is right for everyone, but here is a good guideline:

1. Financial planning should begin early in one's working life stage, probably between ages 30 and 40; issues like investment programs and life insurance should be initiated by then.

2. Initial consideration of retirement options should start between the ages of 40 and 50, when one can begin to think beyond the expenses of raising a family, paying college tuition and finally wrapping up those seemingly never-ending mortgage payments.

3. Major retirement decisions can start in our 50s, when the pursuit of leisure time preferences begins to sharpen our focus, perhaps pointing us toward potential retirement locations or toward investing in a lot or a rental property where we might eventually like to have a retirement home or cottage.

4. Creation of an initial retirement plan / life plan should begin by age 55. It is during this phase that you may begin thinking more seriously about how

you want to invest your time, talent and treasures for God's glory. How has God uniquely called you to serve him? Regular review and adjustment of your plan should occur between ages 55 and 65 (or your target retirement age, if that is earlier).

5. The last year before retirement should include fine-tuning of the plan, taking into account changes that have occurred in your economic situation, family dynamics and other areas of your life that could spur you to adjust your target retirement date, your work plan or your expected lifestyle.

When considering this retirement planning schedule, keep in mind that

1. Every retirement plan is unique; there is no single best template.
2. Retirement is a cyclical process, not a single event in time.
3. Retirement planning is a continuing process that requires frequent review and adjustment.

These points are so important that I will be coming back to them on multiple occasions over the course of the rest of this book.

Retirement Myths

Let's review some common retirement myths. These come about as a result of doing retirement "the old fashioned way." This is the old-paradigm way of thinking about retirement: understanding it as a single point in time when traditional work stops and a new life stage of reduced activity begins. Let's look at some of the common misconceptions and fears associated with this traditional idea.

Retirement Equals an Early Death

Have you ever met anyone who is genuinely fearful of retiring, afraid that this step will be the equivalent of signing their own death warrant? Or have you known someone who retired after many years on the job, only to have their health decline immediately after retiring, ending in an early death? Contrary to this myth, there is no medical, factual connection between retirement and an early death. However, some retirees fail to remain physically and mentally active in retirement and allow their health to deteriorate rapidly, which certainly can lead to premature expiration. But retirement, in and of itself, is not lethal.

The end of a working life does signal a major life shift. However, the wise retiree will have plans in place that will allow them to maintain a mental and physical sharpness so that they can continue to remain engaged in life and find meaning and purpose. The saying (we hear it frequently in a popular television commercial) is that "a body at rest tends to stay at rest, and a body in motion tends to stay in motion." Keeping this in mind, the thoughtful retiree will engage in mental and physical exercise that allows them to stay in the game of life and not just sit on the sidelines.

Retirement Is a Piece of Cake

Some people enter this phase of life with no plan at all. They simply intend to stop working and enjoy life. This may be because their work has been so stressful and their life so hectic that they are simply looking forward to a time of doing very little to nothing at all. Perhaps this was the way they spent their vacations during their working life, and they are now seeing it as their full-time right—to relax, kick back and enjoy life. While extended times of rest may be necessary for some people who have experienced a great deal of stress and anxiety in their work life, this in itself is not a successful plan for transitioning into retirement.

The successful retiree will mix leisure with work. While it's true that individuals who retire typically do take some time off to do some of the things they have always wanted to do—travel, engage in a hobby, work on their retirement home and the like—there comes a time when a life of leisure becomes a life of boredom. The goal is to find meaning and purpose in this new phase of life, not simply to allow leisure to become one's full-time focus. When purposeful tasks are a part of the retiree's regular schedule, the times of leisure become that much more enjoyable.

Retirement Is All about the "Honey Do" List

While this sounds humorous, it is the plan for some in retirement: to finally get around to fixing things around the house or cottage that have long been neglected and are overdue for attention. Some people look up against this phase and put off retirement because they don't want to be a handyman for the rest of their lives, at the beck and call of their spouse to take care of all the little jobs around the house.

Again, it's all about managing expectations and creating a schedule that works for the retiree. Certainly, having time to get work done around the house or a retirement property is a good thing. And using one's skills is one way to stay physically and mentally sharp. However, leaning toward doing only one thing in retirement will lead to an imbalance in the retiree's life; understanding that fact and planning for times of activity mixed in with leisure and other pursuits will allow one's life to maintain a healthy balance.

Retirement Is about Hobbies

This myth is common for those who have a passion for a hobby and believe that if they can spend more time engaged in it they will be happier. This pursuit gives them joy and a sense of satisfaction, and yet it is often not enough to provide ongoing fulfillment and purpose in their life in retirement. Golf, travel, television, fishing, reading, leisure: all of these things eventually become tiresome.

Certainly hobbies are a great way for an individual in retirement to stay physically and mentally sharp. And there's no question that many hobbies can do a lot of good for a lot of people. If one's hobby is working on mechanical devices and fixing small engines or appliances or automobiles, this could benefit friends and family alike. If one's hobby is woodworking, building beautiful pieces of furniture is certainly a way of contributing to society. Either of these endeavors could supply a welcome source of income for the retiree as well. To cite another example, if one has been a career nurse, there are all kinds of ways to volunteer to help people in need of assistance.

These are just a few examples of ways in which sideline interests can become part of a healthy and balanced post-retirement life. How have your vocational or avocational experiences equipped you to contribute to being an active participant within your sphere of influence?

Success in My Career Means Easy Passage

This myth is common among people who have been successful in their working years and believe that transitioning into retirement should lead them into similar success. But the truth is that knowing how to navigate a career is much different from understanding how to reorder one's world to a retirement phase.

When considering retirement, it's helpful to approach this passage as one would who is working on being successful in a career. What are the steps to accomplishment in a career? Having goals, moving proactively toward them, planning ahead, maintaining a consistent and daily focus on the tasks at hand, getting up every day and working toward knocking off items on one's to-do list, and the like. If a retiree lives for 20 or 30 years post-retirement, that next phase of life deserves all of the careful planning, proactivity and consistency that went into the career phase.

Retirement Means It's Someone Else's Turn Now

This take on the issue is likely to come from those who have been fully and actively engaged during their work years in outside activities, such as in a church or some other volunteer setting. Their lives have been so busy with their career and other pursuits that as they approach retirement they are experiencing a burnout phase. They desire to unplug from all the activity, believing that leaving these tasks to others will give them respite and happiness.

As we've seen with many of these other myths, this new phase of life must involve careful planning and a mix of work and leisure. Rest is a part of the mix, without question, and perhaps pulling back from a full schedule of work and volunteer activities is warranted. But you might want to consider what role you could play as a mentor to others who are moving into these volunteer positions. How could you be active in passing the torch to a new generation of individuals who are willing to take it up and move forward? Consider the value of your experience and expertise before deciding to abruptly leave behind all of the activities that were once a part of your daily life. A phased approach to being relieved of some responsibility so that leisure time can become a part of your weekly schedule is often the best course of action.

Retirement Will Allow Me to Stay Busy, But at My Own Pace

This myth says that "if I just stay busy, I will have a very happy retirement." Indeed, it is possible for people transitioning into retirement to be very busy. There are lots of undertakings—involvement with the kids or grandkids, community activities, leisure activities and simply chores around the house—that can easily take up one's day, but do these provide meaning and purpose?

That's the most important question to ask when addressing the retirement years: Will simply staying busy be enough to satisfy my desire to remain engaged in the world around me and influential within my social circles? Again, finding meaning and purpose requires a detailed analysis of one's interests and abilities in order to find one's true calling in the post-career years. This requires careful planning and a deep understanding of what brings satisfaction and fulfillment. What do you have to contribute to the people around you? What wisdom or skill can you teach to another that will allow that person to improve his or her life or surroundings? How can you influence others in a positive way, using the talents and abilities you have? Generally speaking, maintaining this kind of others focus is a good way to find meaning and purpose in life.

Retirement Is Like One Long Vacation

Vacations are a fun and enjoyable time for almost everyone. This is especially true when one is working full-time and engaged in productive but stressful activities from which one needs a respite. A vacation is a wonderful break from a busy and active schedule, but can a "permanent vacation" provide the same experience as a true vacation during one's working years?

The thought that retirement should be a permanent vacation can mislead those who are transitioning into this life stage if they are unaware of the pitfalls. By its very definition a vacation is "an extended period of recreation, especially one spent away from home or in traveling." As we've discussed above, a period of travel and leisure can be a healthy part of one's early retirement, and planning for other periods of similar activity can be a fun and rewarding way to keep one's energy and motivation high during retirement. However, travel tends to be expensive, and as one gets older the experience can be wearying. For these and many other reasons, incorporating travel into one's life as part of a planned portfolio of activities that includes both times of work and of rest is a solid approach to retirement.

While there seem to be elements of truth in all of these myths, they all point to an imbalanced approach to retirement. Focusing too much on any one thing can turn retirement into drudgery, so building a plan for mixing in work, leisure, travel, time spent with family and friends, and meaningful volunteer activities will allow the prepared retiree to enjoy life for many years. Such a plan takes vision and an understanding of one's desires, talents and abilities, as well as of one's physical and financial capacities. However, creating and executing a plan based on a long-term vision is the best approach to keeping life interesting and fulfilling in retirement.

5

Options for Retirement

In this chapter I want to summarize all that we've discussed to this point and take a look at different options we can pursue in retirement. Here I want to lay out
and define some of the various options available for our
retirement years. Many different models for retirement
have been promoted, and we need to take a look at them
in light of what Scripture tells us about our life choices.
The first model we'll look at is pure leisure; the second a
mixture of work and leisure; the third a mixture of time
spent volunteering and leisure; the fourth full-time work;
and the final, fifth model a combination of the first four.

Pure Leisure

Let's think about the pure leisure paradigm for retirement. Certainly this is a model that sounds appealing to a harried career worker who is stressed out and ready to leave the daily grind for a more relaxed phase of life. But is this a biblical approach to retirement? Does Scripture anywhere advise us that it is recommended, advisable or even allowable for us spend our waning years simply relaxing and focusing on making ourselves happy?

For those of us who are familiar with the Bible, the answer is a relatively obvious no. The pursuit of a life of self-interest is not part of a biblical worldview. Does this mean that pursuing any kind of leisure is wrong? Absolutely not! Leisure is an important part of our life in retirement; it helps to keep us energized, revitalized, restored and renewed. But leisure accomplishes its goals only if it is balanced by times of engaged and purposeful activity. Surely God wants us to enjoy a life that is less hectic and less driven than what we have experienced during our career. We can certainly enjoy times of leisure with our family and friends. But God also wants us to follow him, to be generous with what he has given us and to use our talents in furthering his kingdom cause. If we follow God, our natural impulse will be to serve him by serving others.

What leisure activities are available to us in retirement? Let's look at the most obvious: retirement homes or cottages, educational pursuits, arts and culture, sports and fitness, common interest groups and entertainment. Any or all of these can all have an important place in our retirement years.

If you have planned well, perhaps there is a place to which you can retire, a home or cottage near a recreational waterway that allows you to pursue your interests in golf, fishing, boating or other activities. Such a place can be a wonderful gathering point for family and friends and a key part of your satisfaction and enjoyment in retirement. With this kind of situation, as with all others, the key is finding ways to maximize the use of such a place so that the most people can benefit from it. Can your church youth group come up for a day? Perhaps you can offer a long weekend at the cottage as part of a silent auction as a benefit to some charity? How else can you make use of such a location to improve the lives of others through your generous hospitality?

Next, let's look at education. There are many opportunities to continue our education, even in our later years of life. This may sound odd, given that education is usually thought of as a way of preparing us in our early years for our future life and career. But the truth is that education can and should be a life-long process, affording us opportunities to improve our skills and keep our minds sharp. While acquiring new skills can be fun and exciting, doing so can also be useful as we age, equipping us with new abilities for new opportunities. Home improvement projects, for example, provide us with occasions to practice new skills.

Do you have a love of "life-long learning"? Is this a part of who you are and who you want to be? Do you read and study to improve your knowledge base and keep your mind engaged and challenged? Of what opportunities will you take advantage? For example, you could take a class in Spanish to learn basic Spanish skills, then study a region of the world where Spanish is the primary language and finally travel there to experience that area, as well as to use the language skills you've acquired. Exercising the kind of vision that would move you along a timeline from learning the language to studying the region to planning the trip to actually getting on a plane would keep your motivation strong and your mind and heart engaged.

Exploring culture is another opportunity you might want to pursue in your leisure time. Many communities have vital, in-depth culture and arts organizations. Civic theater, local symphony performances, opera, ballet, museums and other cultural exploration opportunities can be an exciting component of the retirement years. We may finally have the time and motivation to enjoy being involved as a patron, a participant or a volunteer for one or more of these organizations.

Sports and fitness are another important area to explore during this phase of life. Not only are these activities good for our health but also for the fun and camaraderie afforded by engaging in them with other people. The opportunity to learn new or to develop latent skills in which we have an interest in (e.g., in golf or tennis or fly fishing) can be valuable in the pursuit of a healthier lifestyle.

Quite often the organizations that cater to seniors and encourage a more active lifestyle offer reduced rates for beginner classes so that seniors can explore the different options available without investing a lot of money, time or energy.

Joining common interest groups is another way of continuing our growth and development in retirement. We may opt to join literary clubs, gardening clubs, recreational clubs or music groups. All of these can align with our specific interests to provide the enjoyment and social connections that become more and more important in our retirement years.

Finally, we can pursue leisure through various entertainment related options. There are many opportunities of which seniors can take advantage to enjoy different versions of entertainment. Interesting and educational television series, concerts, plays and sporting events that run the gamut from youth to high school to college to professional are only a few of the possibilities in this area. Even taking the time to go out and enjoy a movie every now and then can add richness and fun to this next stage of life.

Work and Leisure

A combination of work and leisure may make the most sense for many people. Rather than an exclusive focus on leisure, the individual may choose to blend work and leisure in this stage of life. As we've noted previously in this book, the working life brings many benefits to us as we pursue our careers, and maintaining at least some of these can do us good us as we move ahead into retirement.

Is there an opportunity in conjunction with your employer for you to gradually reduce the number of hours you work to afford increased opportunities to pursue more leisure and service activities? If not, is there some other position you can pursue that will give you the kind of flexibility you're looking for, while also maintaining some of the economic and social benefits available in the working world?

As we consider such a combination of work and leisure, it is important to keep in mind the importance of pursuing a life of service. As believers we need to follow Jesus' model for living. It is critical for us to understand that, no matter where we find ourselves in this situation, our focus ought not to be solely on our work or leisure but ultimately on helping to build up God's kingdom on the earth. If we continue to work as part of our retirement, we need to determine which of these benefits we can use to help other people. If we work for financial gain, how can we use that to serve others?

Volunteering and Leisure

If one's situation is such that relative financial stability is in place, then working as a volunteer can be most rewarding during this phase. Consider whether you will work for pay or as a volunteer to gain other benefits of work without the financial remuneration. The opportunity to do what one loves while serving others and giving back is an exciting challenge to which many retirees look forward. This also makes the work less demanding because the volunteer is *choosing* to work versus being *required* to work.

In the area of volunteer work, there are many options available. It is important to explore those opportunities that are best aligned with our interests and passions so that the experience will be as enjoyable and rewarding as possible. There are secular volunteer opportunities, e.g., within local arts or community organizations. There are also faith-based opportunities, which may align better with your values of building up God's kingdom.

Of course, if you are already involved in a church or ministry, it's likely that you'll want to increase your volunteer hours there. If you'd like to find out what else is available, ask your pastor or close friends who spend their time volunteering what they enjoy doing. Habitat for Humanity may not be for everyone; nor would volunteering in a hospital helping patients find their way. The point is that very few organizations will reach out to you and ask for your time.

Realize that you now have the opportunity to decide exactly how you will spend your time and energy, so take your time and do your research before you make any long-term volunteer commitments. Try several out for a half-day or for a week. Or choose more than one, and vary your schedule and activities to keep your mind fresh and to be involved in a larger variety of activities.

Whatever our choice for this phase of life, it is important to seek God's call on our life so that we understand his expectation for how we can most effectively utilize our time, talents and treasures.

Full-Time Work

For some retirees a combination of work along with both volunteering and leisure is not an option. For financial reasons, or for any number of the social and purpose-driven aspects of remaining in a full-time position, many seniors decide to rejoin the workforce. For those who have the energy, motivation and stamina to do so, choosing another full-time job after one's "first retirement" is the best and most fulfilling path to finding purpose and meaning in life.

Is full-time work for you? Have you tried to relax and enjoy life and failed to find fulfillment? Is your financial situation such that you need to pursue a different career at this point in your life? If so, take your time to find out what type of position best meshes with the talents with which you've been blessed. Is there a career path you can take that will allow you more flexible hours? Is there perhaps something you could do at home that would keep your mind interested and engaged, such as freelance editorial or design work? After a long career in a challenging industry, is there a way you could consult for a living and enjoy the travel and exploration that come with such a career change? The advantage of returning to the workforce after one's initial retirement is that there is often time to study and learn about the various options available before moving ahead. If full-time work is for you, take the time to understand your options; shop around and find the best place for you to fit back in to the workforce.

Combination Approach

This last approach to retirement planning and focus is a simple combination of any and all of the above. An excellent approach to this involves looking at your schedule and deciding what you want to do with your time. Do you have a need to bring in at least some income? Then pursue part-time work in a place that you think you would enjoy. Are there grandchildren that you'd like to spend more time with? Work with your kids to schedule those times—a clear, well-defined schedule can do wonders for stopping the creeping scope of these responsibilities that sometimes happens.

Is there an organization to which you'd like to devote some of your time? Manage their expectations and give them the hours that you feel you can reasonably give, so that you don't lose the opportunity to spend time doing the other activities you truly enjoy. Do you have a property that you want to use more than you did in your working years? Be sure you can get full weeks off of your part-time or volunteer activities so that you can enjoy time with friends and family.

This combination approach has many benefits. It keeps us interested; it brings fulfillment; it allows us to enjoy the things that we have worked hard for; it gives us a sense of activity and purpose without being too stressful; and it allows us to manage our own schedules, rather than having them managed for us. Envision, if you will, a glass jar. Next to it is a small pile of rocks and a bucket of sand. If the glass jar is your schedule and all of your activities (the rocks and sand) have to fit in that jar, where will you begin?

If you pour the sand in first (represented by schedule creep, last-minute opportunities or demands, email, social networking and the like), then there will be no room for the rocks in the jar (the important activities that you really want to include in your week). Plan to put the big rocks in first, then pour the sand around them. That's the only way that all of these things will fit. Schedule your activities in such a way as to ensure that your most treasured priorities take precedence over the rest of what happens during the course of a normal week.

In all of this, remember, as we discussed in the introduction and first chapter of this book, retirement for the baby boomer generation is cyclical. For many there will be periods of part-time or full-time work, times of leisure, opportunities to volunteer one's time and talents, and chances to pursue other interests. As you approach your retirement years, make sure you spend time looking into all your options and understand that this possibly long period of time will likely include seasons when your interests and abilities will morph and develop as you take advantage of new opportunities and challenges and as friends and family open you up to new vistas of life.

6

Purpose-Filled Retirement

As we've seen from the previous chapters, the goal of a successful retirement is finding one's purpose and pursuing it. This final chapter will take a look at multiple aspects of one's retirement years, taking into consideration how one can go about finding purpose and meaning in a post-career life.

Our first challenge is to assess our state of preparedness for transitioning into retirement. In order to examine this more closely, we will be focusing on six life areas associated with retirement that I have found to be critical when I advise my clients on this next phase of life. In order to experience a successful retirement, one must fully develop these particular arenas of life:

1. Career and work
2. Health and wellness
3. Financial preparedness
4. Family and relationships
5. Leisure and social activities
6. Personal development

Career and work have to do with our degree of satisfaction and fulfillment in our current career, in light of our personality. As we look at this first critical category, we will examine three aspects of this life arena: ideal work, work benefits and work options.

Health and wellness has to do with the degree to which we are physically, mentally and spiritually prepared for this phase of our life. In this section we will examine our inner self, looking at our self-concept, our self-confidence and our self-esteem. How healthy is our concept of self, and how attuned are we to who we are and what we're about? Our actual physical and mental wellness is, to a large degree, impacted by life factors over which we exert significant control. How well are you doing in this area as you approach retirement?

The next phase is *financial preparedness*. Our financial readiness is one of the critical factors in our retirement years, and having a solid financial plan in place is a foundation for a successful and enjoyable retirement. Financial security can protect against unhappiness, but having this security doesn't necessarily lead to happiness. Taking responsibility for understanding the financial issues that affect retirement, and doing the necessary planning to achieve financial confidence in retirement, often require professional assistance from someone who is qualified to advise you on these challenges and reflect with you on the opportunities.

Family and relationships are important because our interrelations within our family and social network have a significant impact on our happiness and satisfaction in any phase of our life. Working in this area is important because any existing problems in our family relationships can be compounded in retirement, when there is more time to ponder our life and the status of these interactions. It's often true that if problems exist in these relationships before retirement they will be magnified by additional time spent in close proximity during one's retirement years. Because of this, it's vitally important to do the hard work of uncovering and solving the problems and issues before moving on to the next life phase. If we find ourselves dealing in retirement with these continued challenges, it's imperative for us to get help to work on improving these relationships.

Other family issues that can positively or negatively affect one's retirement include caring for aging parents, caring for dependent children (even adult children), caring for grandchildren or being responsible for others in retirement. Family and close friends can provide much-needed companionship, conversation and support (sometimes including financial support) as we progress through our retirement years, and the strength of these relationships is most often determined well in advance of retirement.

Leisure and social activities often become a significantly larger factor in retirement than in pre-retirement. Leisure activity can be broadly defined as "what you do when you don't have anything you have to do," which in retirement includes many types of activities: family time, volunteering, education, travel, sports, arts and culture, physical exercise and many other options. Leisure includes both time spent with others and time spent alone. What will you do when you find you have time on your hands?

Finally, *personal development* is an important aspect of this life phase. It's all about bringing meaning to your life by pursuing your dreams and cementing your purpose. Having a life purpose provides a framework for our mental, emotional and spiritual satisfaction and stimulates our hope for the future. This includes exercising our minds by continuing to gain knowledge, which can be achieved in various ways. Continuing education, for example, can develop personal strength and talents, transform interests into endeavors and provide stimulating social interaction. Personal development can also be enhanced through volunteering. A life pattern of giving back to society heightens our zest for life and even enhances life expectancy, per a recent University of Michigan study. It positively impacts our attitudes, values and beliefs and fosters gratefulness for the blessings we have enjoyed throughout our life. As many volunteers will attest, "giving is receiving."

Career and Work Options

There are three components of career and work:

1. Ideal work — What type of work is best suited for you, in either your pre- or post-retirement years?

2. Work benefits — The physical, financial and emotional needs filled by your work are many, so how effectively you replace these benefits in retirement is key to finding happiness in this phase of life.

3. Work options — What work structure will best suit your retirement plan? Will full-time work, part-time work for pay, self-employment, volunteer work or maybe some combination be the best for you in the long run?

Ideal Work

To dig into this a little more deeply, let's start by understanding that there are various work personalities. It is important to understand your own so you can align your career with your personality.

Realistic. People who have a realistic type of work personality characteristically choose careers that involve physical activity, manual skill jobs, athletic activities or working with objects, tools or machines. Oftentimes this kind of career involves working with machinery or plants or animals or working out-of-doors.

Conventional. This second type of work personality is best suited to working with data or information using clerical or numerical skills and abilities and either creating or following guidelines, structures and operating procedures. This kind of work attracts people who are more detail-oriented and possess an ability to follow through in an organized fashion.

Enterprising. This third work personality is embodied by those who enjoy working with people, have skills that allow them to influence and persuade others and enjoy performing or making presentations. People with this personality may have leadership capabilities, and those who are enterprising often enjoy developing and building an organization on the basis of their managerial and leadership skills.

Social. The social work personality is characterized by people who have strong communication skills, an ability to instruct or teach and effective human relations skills. These individuals have a high emotional intelligence and are able to think quickly on their feet. Typified by someone who works in customer service or customer relations, such people have a firm grasp of the knowledge base required for their job and know how to make the consumer happy.

Artistic. This type of work personality is characterized by skills and abilities in innovation, creation, ability to conceptualize and design, and competence in crafting something beautiful out of raw materials in music or art or some physical medium.

Investigative. This last work personality is characterized by analysis, problem solving, honing key observational skills, and effective decision making. Such individuals thrive where there are problems to be solved, material to be sifted through and compared and analyzed, and decisions to be made.

As you think about these six personality types, which do you feel is closest to your area of competence or satisfaction? Which best defines you? Which type of personality would you identify as your sweet spot, both for your working career and for your retirement? As you consider these six work personalities, think about which one, or which mix of them, best defines what you do in your career now and what you might wish to do in the future. This is the best way to identify and begin to understand the best match for your retirement years.

Understand, too, that there may be some switching back and forth among the six different personality types at different life stages of your journey. Perhaps the advent of your retirement will move you from a conventional work personality to an artistic one as you engage your passion for a craft or some other artistic pursuit. After a while you may want to focus on the more social aspects of your work and life environment. The point is that having knowledge at our disposal of these six different types of work personalities will allow us to plan more comprehensively and effectively than we may have done in the past. If we know which of these have characterized us in the past and which we would like to move toward, we can be more intentional as we envision ourselves physically moving from one to the other.

While one work personality might have characterized us in the past, it doesn't necessarily have to characterize us in the same way in the future. Please take a few minutes to review the list again and think about these questions:

1. Does my past or current career fit well with my work personality?

2. If so, how will continuing in the niche for that personality type work for me in the future?

3. If not, how will making a conscious switch to employment calling for a different personality type open new doors of opportunity for me?

4. If my career and work personality are consistent, is there another work personality to which I might also aspire?

5. If so, what are the concrete action steps I can take to help move me in this direction?

Work Benefits

Stop for a minute and think about the benefits you derive from the work you do. Of course, income is a key driver in that list, but it may not be the first one you consider. Work gives us a sense of identity; gets us dressed and out of the house; provides consistent, if not daily socialization; helps us with our time management; and can provide a keen sense of purpose.

As we think about all these benefits, it's important that we recognize that when we retire we will experience a potentially dramatic change in many of these areas. This is why many people who come to the end of their careers at their "first retirement" look for another opportunity to pursue. Recognizing that many of these work benefits are soon to change, they choose a work option for retirement that involves finding an ongoing position in order to maintain some of the benefits of work.

Considering the work personalities outlined above, think for a minute about what kind of work you've done in the past and what kind of work you might like to do in the future. If you owned a landscaping company, would you be willing to do work that involves sitting at a desk, or would you prefer to continue working outdoors? If you were in a position that brought daily interaction with the public, would you rather pursue one that allows you to focus more on a smaller group of people or that perhaps keeps you away from public interaction altogether?

Pursuing other work after finalizing one's career is not an uncommon occurrence among first retirees today. Quite often their skills, experience and knowledge lead them to rewarding work that is different from what their main career might have been; in other situations they will gravitate toward the same kind of career, as it fits well with their work personality and interest. The key here is to recognize that the benefits of a working life are varied and valuable and to understand that finding a replacement for these is an important aspect toward finding fulfillment in retirement.

Work Options

Perhaps one of the greatest benefits of being in a strong financial position when heading into retirement is that we can pick and choose what we will do in our continuing work life. So let's consider the various work options we may have as we move into this next phase of life.

Think about the career you have just left or will soon leave. As you map out your next phase of life and think about the activities you have planned, which work structure will best suit your retirement plan? Is there an industry in which you have always wanted to work that might be a possibility for you now? Say you owned a business but also pursued a certificate to become a master gardener. Would it be fulfilling to you to work at a nursery with a retail store where you would be able to pursue your passion for plants, as well as help others as they pursue the kind of beauty you have found? If so, which would work best for you: full-time or part-time work? What about working evenings and Saturdays? Are you willing to do either?

Or say you have spent a lifetime in the employ of another person or organization and would like to move out on your own. Is there an option for self-employment that would bring the same kinds of satisfaction you found in your previous career? Perhaps you have a friend or relative who is self-employed who could benefit from your skill and knowledge. Many people never think about this, but self-employment can be incredibly fulfilling as one is allowed to set all of his or her own timelines, work schedules and product releases.

Perhaps volunteer work seems better suited to your retirement interests. If so, is there some organization for which you have a particular affinity that you would like to approach as a potential volunteer? Perhaps a church organization, an adoption agency, a political platform or party or a veteran's facility. Take a minute to write down a short list of such organizations.

We've taken a quick look at full-time work, part-time work, self-employment and volunteer opportunities. Which one of these will fit you best as you look toward the next phase of life? Will it be one of these or perhaps a combination that will keep you interested and engaged in the long run?

Health and Wellness

Health and wellness are significant factors for our retirement years. Factors that affect longevity include lifestyle, environment and heredity. It is important that we factor all of these into our plan for longevity and retirement. The first step in all of this, of course, is a comprehensive annual physical with one's doctor. It seems as though this most basic factor would hardly bear a mention, but I've met many people who have simply put off doctor visits for many years. If this is you, as a first step schedule an appointment with your doctor and then make sure to follow through on his or her instructions. Heading into retirement requires a comprehensive assessment of one's financial, social, spiritual and emotional aspects, but please don't neglect the physical.

As they approach retirement, too many people underestimate the number of retirement years for which they will need to plan because they are relying on outdated statistics or are making invalid assumptions. For instance, "My parents didn't live that long, so I probably won't either." Such a statement needs to take into account the variables that advances in disease treatment and modern medicine can provide. If your parents' lifestyle was significantly different from your own, take into account the factors that could make your life a lot longer than those your parents enjoyed. The key here is planning for the long term while still enjoying the day-to-day.

One of the key variables with regard to health is our health practices. It is very important that we understand the factors of health and the variables we can control and influence. The top ten health problems in our country today are all behaviorally affected. These include heart disease, stroke, pneumonia and influenza, cancer, respiratory diseases, diabetes, septicemia, injuries, Alzheimer's disease and kidney disease. Ask your doctor how you can avoid some of the more common causes of these top ten factors and what you need to do to keep your mind and body sharp.

Other skills we need to factor in with regard to our overall health and wellness are as follows:

1. Assertiveness: Are we being proactive and assertive in managing our own health? Are we doing the right research, asking the right questions of our health care providers and working to manage our own conditions? Do we know what effect the medications we're taking may have on our day-to-day health, and are we self-aware enough to understand that we may need a change in our medications in order to feel and function better? Assertiveness can move us a long way toward maintaining our long-term health. Managing one's own care is critical in this information age.

2. Establishing priorities: Are we making the right choices each day when it comes to the amount of exercise we get, the kinds of foods we eat, the kinds of activities in which we engage, and other such choices? Helpful in this analysis will be the creation of a *written* list of priorities. One can hardly keep to a program if there is no written documentation outlining one's goals and consistently reminding us of what we have previously agreed to. Build your schedule around these priorities as a way to maintain your health, and you'll find that you're much less likely to crowd out these kinds of activities when other opportunities arise. For example, "I want to walk 30 minutes 5 days a week, eat 4 fruits and 4 vegetables a day, sleep 8 hours every night, do one activity to sharpen my mental focus (i.e., read a novel or do Sudoku or a crossword puzzle), and see my doctor once every 6 months." These are simple, doable priorities that will motivate you to get up in the morning and allow you to build some structure into your day.

3. Know your own body: This step involves understanding discomfort, whether it is physical or emotional. As far as our own bodies are concerned, knowing our aches and

pains and discovering what to do in response to them is critical in assessing our long-term health. We also need to recognize and analyze when a relationship or some other situation is causing us emotional or mental pain and when these factors need to be addressed in our life. The key here is being as self-aware as we can possibly be; knowing our strengths, weaknesses and what motivates or demotivates us; and then acting to correct any of the negatives we can.

4. Resolving old conflicts: Related to the above, this one is of key importance, especially when it involves forgiveness. As we know from much psychological study, the act of forgiving, or of withholding forgiveness, can have significant physical, mental and emotional effects on our bodies. Is there an old grudge you need to resolve? Someone in your life you've hurt who needs to hear from you that you're sorry? Someone who has hurt you who needs to know what effect that pain has had on your life? As we've stated earlier, the emotional baggage you carry through life will only be magnified when you take it with you into retirement. Make positive steps today to understand

what these issues are and, if you need to, to get help to work them out. You'll be better off for exploring what makes you tick and what may be standing in the way of your overall physical and emotional health.

5. Maintaining a sense of humor: Sometimes a shift to a new life stage brings with it a sense of stoicism, as we move ahead into the unknown. But the most successful people in retirement will be able to approach the coming issues and problems as opportunities to be explored and life events to be enjoyed. Is your glass half-full or half-empty? Do you tend toward optimism or pessimism? When something negative happens, is your first response negative or positive? How do you understand the role of God's plan on your life? It has been said that bad things don't happen *to* you but *for* you. If you can approach your life with a sense of humor, with an attitude that says "No matter what, I'm not going to let this get me down" and learning from what life throws at you, you'll have moved a long way toward maintaining the kind of attitude that will take you positively into whatever life change you find yourself facing.

6. Finding your spiritual source: As we approach a time in our lives when we will have opportunity to slow down somewhat, to enjoy a quieter pace and to relax, it's good to spend some time reflecting on the source of our spiritual well-being. For me as a Christian, my sense of God's control over my life gives me the kind of assurance that money simply can't buy. When I think of the salvation I have on the basis of Christ's life, death and resurrection, this colors every aspect of my life and my every interaction with other people. It spurs me on to generosity, to imitating the God who is all about love. That gives me hope and perspective on my life as a whole. When we pursue these spiritual truths in our retirement, we find a richness and perspective that perhaps has been long neglected because of career constraints. Whatever your religious affiliation, take the time to explore what affords you peace. This is a critical aspect of self-awareness that also affects self-worth and self-image—all important aspects of the current discussion.

As we consider these various health-related factors, a valid question we need to ask ourselves is whether we living with vitality. Are we enjoying life? Are we seeking challenge and opportunity? It is critically important to approach these questions with a high level both of self-awareness and of self-regard, to value physical health, to have a high sense of personal worth, to have a strong faith and to expect positivity and success in our lives.

How do we maintain a strong sense of vitality? Consider these different aspects, all of which help foster a holistic approach to a sense of vitality in our lives:

1. Relationships: It is extremely important to have a strong network of relationships in order to maintain vitality. Significant contact with others, be it electronic or in person, is vital to maintaining our sense of self and connectedness to our community. Be it in the neighborhood; at church; within a small social circle of dear, long-term friends; or through some other point of connectedness, having and maintaining relationships with others is critical to the sense of vitality we're examining here. Bear in mind that social isolation rarely delivers benefits.

2. Managing stress: When we come to a self-awareness about the stressors that affect our lives, we can begin to manage them one by one. Is financial stress keeping you awake at night? Perhaps you can pursue help via various professional options. What about physical stress? Sometimes a factor as seemingly innocuous as caffeine can cause stress that is hidden in the background. What other factors contribute to stress in your life: driving during rush hour? Perhaps you can schedule appointments that avoid these times. Shopping for basic necessities? There are myriad online options for ordering basic supplies that simply come to your door month by month, many of which ship free. Does being in a crowded environment bring you stress? Then understand what this does to you and minimize the amount of activity that places you in this situation. Personal awareness is key to managing stress.

3. Using our gifts: We are all created with gifts; God has built into each of us skills, abilities, interests and passions that fuel our excitement and make life enjoyable for us. We need to nurture and perhaps unleash those

interests and passions in order to maintain our vitality. When one is living in one's giftedness and using time and talents in the interest of helping others or creating beauty in the world, work is not work. It's a pleasure, and being around other people who are living in and acting on their giftedness is also a pleasure. Maintaining and using our God-given capabilities is an important factor for our health and wellness.

4. Attitude: As mentioned above, the right attitude is critically important in all phases of life, and this is perhaps even more true as we plan for our retirement. Maintaining a positive, hopeful outlook on life brings one a long way toward a life of health and wellness. When practiced consistently, the power of hope and an attitude of thankfulness are two extraordinary gifts God grants us with which we can begin each day.

5. Expectation: The expectation principal is another important and powerful concept we must master. As we find ourselves in a new life situation, we will need to adapt to changes in our physical, financial, emotional and spiritual positions. When we finally have the time

to consider where we are and how we got here, we will begin to understand what we can expect from the future. Maintaining a positive sense of expectation about the future is one of the key ingredients to managing stress and living with vitality.

6. Boundaries: When we become self-aware—when we know our physical, financial, mental and emotional limits—we can move ahead in our new lives with a renewed sense that our priorities (those we talked about earlier in this chapter) will remain intact. This will help us manage our health and wellness as we learn to say no to opportunities that arise that will force us to deviate from that which is most important to our physical, mental, emotional and spiritual well-being.

With all of these factors in play, ask yourself this question: "Do I approach retirement with positive or negative expectations?" Follow it up with this question: "Have I done enough to set priorities so that my whole self will be taken into account and so that I can execute appropriate self-care through the establishment of a consistent routine that will allow me to be flexible while still taking into account what is most important to me?" Again, allow me to stress the importance of drafting a written list of your priorities and placing it in a location where you can see it every day (such as on the bathroom mirror or the refrigerator).

Too often people conceive of retirement as a time of fun, relaxation and idleness. While this may sound attractive when we are busy and our days are filled with stress and craziness, it is not a recipe for true happiness and fulfillment. And, more importantly, it is not biblical. God calls us to a very different experience in all aspects of our life, including our retirement!

Financial Preparedness

Our financial preparedness is another very important piece of retirement. Having the knowledge, doing the planning and having confidence that we have done our best to prepare for retirement is a critical component for retirement success. I have spent my entire career helping people to plan for their financial well-being and assuring them that they can do this, whether they start in their 30s or in their 50s.

Financially speaking, retirement is often described as an "incoming age." This term refers to the life stage in which we need to draw income that is sustainable, predictable and increasing over time to fund the lifestyle we hope to achieve. Ideally, what we're looking for is enough money to fund the lifestyle that will allow us to serve God within the giftedness he has provided, to take advantage of opportunities to serve him both at home and elsewhere.

There are many retirement risks of which we need to be aware. First, the risks connected with longevity are increasing as we live longer because, by and large, people are making better lifestyle choices, maintaining better lifestyle habits and enjoying the benefits of better healthcare. Second, investments carry risk, and in today's environment it is important to be an investor rather than just a saver. Working with a professional advisor to make your money work for you is a critical aspect in maintaining this kind of financial vitality. Third, consumption and taxation are two more risks we need to face and manage in order to effectively fund our retirement years. Have you worked out a monthly budget? Have you planned well for life's inevitable ups and downs (such as car repairs, appliance failures and the like)? Are you appropriately insured? Do you understand how the tax code is going to affect you as you begin to use your saved principal to cover your life expenses? These and many others are factors that will contribute to your sense of vitality as you move into retirement. Again, knowledge of these various factors and an appropriate, consistent approach to investigating them is critical to your financial success and well-being as a retiree.

Income and Flexibility

Let's think of the sources of income as it relates to retirement. More and more people are choosing to maintain work income in retirement to supplement other sources, which are Social Security, pensions, investments, annuities and gifts or inheritances. Do you have a solid sense of what your needs will be? You might want to review the section above as it relates to the kind of work you may want to pursue in retirement, whether to replace some of your income or some of the benefits of the workplace. What are your various income streams, and will those be reliable into the future?

One of the key components of financial success in retirement is to work with a professional to develop a flexible financial retirement plan. We all know that life is neither constant nor consistent; it throws many curves at us, and we need to adapt in order to be successful. One of the keys to managing this phase is to work with a competent and qualified retirement planning specialist who can help you analyze various scenarios and give you excellent guidance toward your goals and objectives. Again, the help and perspective you need is just a phone call and an appointment away. As someone who works in this industry, I can tell you that the peace of mind I can supply to individuals who are less than financially secure is immense and appreciated. The main task of professionals like me is to help people set financial priorities that will maximize their financial resources over the long term.

Family and Relationships

The next area on which we want to focus is that of family and relationships. As we've discussed earlier, any issues that are already present in relationships are likely to be magnified, not marginalized, in retirement. A critical component in facing a long and healthy retirement is understanding the complexities of your relationships and making sure they are healthy as you move into the next phase.

Spouses

The most important relationship for most retirees is their spouse. This relationship is key for most people because they will be spending more time with their husband or wife than with any other person during their retirement. This relationship is often complicated by the fact that, with busy work schedules and family lives, this is the one relationship that may have been damaged or may have deteriorated due to unaddressed conflict that has developed.

In transitioning into retirement it's critically important to spend the time to repair the spousal relationship, or to intentionally build or develop it as needed. For most people this involves working with a competent counselor who will be able to frame the issues and guide the couple through any past hurts or neglect. The goal is to approach the counseling in a positive way that looks toward repairing the foundations of the marriage and developing a long-term plan for happiness and unity.

While it may be difficult to ask for help, quite often the spouses' blind spots can render any discussion between the two less than productive. As with any piece of machinery, we may at times need a professional to "look under the hood" and determine what, if any, tuning needs to occur, either to stave off potential damage or to correct an existing problem. Professional counselors have at their disposal multiple tools that will help to assess the strength of the marriage and address any areas of concern that need to be managed. Essential characteristics of a healthy marital relationship include mutuality, respect, communication, intimacy, trust and commitment. As you approach any counseling situation, make sure these top six aspects are a key part of any discussion.

Parents

For more and more retirees, a critical factor in the family dynamic is aging parents. More and more of the baby boomer generation is feeling pinched between caring for their parents and maintaining their continuing responsibility to provide for their children. Boomers in this situation are often referred to as the "sandwich generation," and the financial and commitment stresses in this situation can be serious. Again, setting boundaries and managing expectations are critical to navigating this phase of retirement.

If you're a member of a larger family that is dealing with aging parents, make sure there is open communication between you, your parents and your siblings or other involved caretakers or decision makers. As you help your parents maintain their lifestyle in the face of the problems and complications of aging, you'll need to apply some of the same characteristics we've been talking about in other aspects of this chapter: proactivity, assertiveness, creativity and compassion.

Assisting aging parents is an honor. Taking on too much, however, or leaving too much responsibility to another sibling or some other caretaker can upset the delicate balance you're trying to achieve as you approach and establish yourselves in retirement.

Children
As you assess your move toward retirement, consider your relationship with your children. As you manage your financial situation, how do they factor in to what

you're doing with your money? Are there any that need your financial or physical support more than the others? What will you do to maintain equity among your children when it comes to these issues?

In my practice I've seen many very wealthy people who give little thought to what is going to happen with their money after they pass on. They imagine they will give it to their children or grandchildren, but the thought of who will get what and what that will mean in terms of family functioning is given short shrift. Leaving a legacy and helping your children manage your final affairs are issues you can proactively address right now. Again, working with a competent professional is likely the best way to approach this aspect of your retirement life. Having a will is one thing; delineating your specific final wishes and funding those before you approach the end of your life will help you in your long-term relationship with your children, and possibly also in their long-term relationships with each other.

But beyond these financial aspects, what is your relationship with your adult children? Are there hurts that need to be addressed, words that need to be spoken, discussions that need to happen? Family counseling is perfect for this kind of situation. Many parents with whom I work live with the pain of broken relationships with their children. Moving proactively toward your kids with the best interests of the family in mind is the best course of action in this case.

Friends

Finally, the need for close friends is critical for social well-being in retirement. Friends have been called "family of choice," and finding and maintaining these relationships is an essential part of our happiness in retirement.

In a different age and a less mobile society, people who approached retirement had a solid base of friends on which to rely. Long-term friendships from work, church or the neighborhood where they had all raised their kids were the bedrock of bonds that would allow them to move smoothly into retirement. But today's context is much different. In a global economy, the old neighborhood ain't what it used to be. People move in and out as jobs change and tend to leave and join other social institutions on a regular basis. On the flipside of this coin, technology allows us to stay connected via multiple electronic means to friends who choose to live around the globe.

Primary in this discussion of friendship is an axiom we all learned in kindergarten: "To have friends, you need to first be a friend." Maintaining these relationships takes time and effort and sacrifice, and whether one is meeting a group of friends for coffee every Wednesday morning or participating in a group online chat with another set of friends spread across the country or across the globe, maintaining connection takes time, planning and persistence. Again, social isolation rarely brings with it any benefits.

Leisure and Social

Now let's look at the leisure and social aspects of retirement. To be sure, the amount and complexity of social interaction varies between individuals. What's enjoyable, relaxing or engaging to one person may not be so to another. Some characteristics of successful social interaction include relaxation, meaningful connection, enjoyment and fun. Much of our more leisurely social interface occurs during the mutual enjoyment of leisure activities.

But how do we approach the leisure we want to build into our retirement life? The paradox of leisure in this phase of life is that it must remain secondary to our primary life focus. If leisure becomes our primary focus, our chief aim, it loses its ability to refresh us. As we saw in the first chapter in our focus on Jim, playing golf may be enjoyable one or two days a week but may become drudgery if played six days a week (considering my game, it would definitely be painful!).

We all want our friends to join us in our leisure activities. And certainly we make friends when we choose certain such activities. But in this situation, as with all others, we need advance planning and must take a balanced approach so we can maintain a healthy relationship between leisure and other, perhaps more purposeful activities. In thinking about this area, make sure to identify your preferences; your current residential, financial and time management situation; your desire for and love of travel; and your interest in hobbies. Realize that, though friends may try to pull you in various activities, your life has limits, be they financial, health related or based on other priorities taking precedence.

It's certainly true that you "can't do it all," so establish your priorities to effectively navigate this phase of life.

Personal Development

Personal development is critical to maintaining a healthy mental and emotional state of mind in retirement. No matter what stage we find ourselves in, our life is intended to have meaning and purpose. God created us to make a difference. He has blessed us to be a blessing, and he expects us to be good stewards of all we have been blessed with. As you approach this new phase of life, make it your goal both to serve and to continue to personally grow and develop, following a path of self-improvement and self-sacrifice that includes education, volunteering and ministry.

True meaning in life comes from the pursuit of activities that give us purpose. We have a sense or feeling that our life is on target when we are engaged in following a calling or purpose. To their detriment, too many people enter the retirement phase without a sense that they should continue to grow and learn. When they lack this call or purpose, they may tend to drift into a life of meaninglessness and emptiness.

Education

Continuing education can be an important component of this phase of life. Local liberal arts colleges and community colleges offer many resources to allow retirees to continue to learn and grow in their knowledge and abilities. In addition, school districts typically offer coursework through community education classes that encourage fitness, knowledge and skill development.

Education can involve pursuing either intellectual or more practical skill development. When we challenge our minds and bodies through continuing to pursue this kind of education, it can be intellectually stimulating, promote good health, improve our skills, expand our interests and simply help us maintain a love of learning. Challenging the mind through learning new skills is the best way to keep it healthy, sharp and engaged.

As you look into these various options, ask your friends what opportunities they have taken advantage of. Call your local colleges, YMCA and community foundations to find out what kinds of courses they offer. Gather all the information you can so you can make an informed choice about the best way to spend your time in pursuing a continuing educational experience.

Volunteering

Volunteering can be another way to maintain vitality in retirement. Volunteers report feelings of increased well-being, heightened motivation to engage with life and increased overall energy. They also report a greater sense of calmness, greater self-worth and fewer aches and pains. The cause of all these benefits is clear: when we volunteer we live beyond ourselves and find focus and fulfillment in improving the lives of other people.

Where can you volunteer your time? Is there a local hospital where you can volunteer to escort patients to the places they need to be? Or could you volunteer at the hospital's nursery to hold babies who have medical difficulties? Can you serve in a more engaged way at your church, perhaps by teaching a class of children or offering to be a part of a hospitality committee? Are there community foundations, political organizations, food banks, charity resale shops or other places where you can donate a portion of your time?

When looking to volunteer a portion of your time, take the time to analyze your strengths and weaknesses. For example, if you've spent your career behind a computer and have never owned your own home, perhaps swinging a hammer and setting drywall in a Habitat for Humanity house isn't the right match for you. Again, the idea here is that you can take the time to select the charity or organization that can help you maximize your talents and abilities. Then again, it doesn't hurt to try something you think might stretch and challenge you to grow and improve your skill set. Whatever you decide, approach it with an open mind to take advantage of the opportunities, but also understand that there's no dishonor in trying something and deciding it isn't for you.

Spirituality

Retirement can become a phase of life in which we explore our spirituality in a more robust way. A reduced schedule can allow us to pursue a path toward greater spirituality as we spend time in small groups and other contexts in which we can explore our spiritualty. When we do so, this activity can and will direct our retirement path.

An increased focus on the more spiritual aspects of our lives will allow us a greater vision of life beyond ourselves, of directing our lives toward a greater purpose than mere self-interest and self-actualization. Our motivation to work, volunteer and enjoy leisure activities is heavily dependent upon our relationship with God and our willingness to follow his call.

Discerning our spiritual gifts will give us the opportunity to fully steward all that he has given us—our time, talents and treasure—during this phase of life. There are many resources on the subject of spiritually directed retirement planning, including many excellent books that have been written on this subject.

Conclusion

The goal of retirement, as we've said so often in this book, is *balance*. As you pursue different opportunities in your retirement life, be sure to maintain a sense of following what you see as your top priorities for your own personal health and well-being. Set boundaries around your time and efforts so you will not become overcommitted; understand your limitations and your strengths; listen to your body and maintain your health at all costs; and pursue the kind of spirituality that will provide you with purpose and direction as you move forward in life.

God has created you in a way that uniquely ties in to his plan for the world. Now that you're facing retirement, you can begin to pursue the kinds of activities that will allow you to maximize your time, talents and treasure in the interest of others. Finding a higher purpose and calling includes tapping in to your passions and proclivities in a way that will allow you to truly thrive in this next phase of life.

> Command those who are rich in this present world not to be arrogant nor to put their hope in wealth, which is so uncertain, but to put their hope in God, who richly provides us with everything for our enjoyment. Command them to do good, to be rich in good deeds, and to be generous and willing to share. In this way they will lay up treasure for themselves as a firm foundation for the coming age, so that they may take hold of the life that is truly life. (1 Timothy 6:17–19)